MAY   2017

"**Great** things in business are **never** done by one person, they are done by **a team of people**."

— **Steve Jobs**

We asked:

What is your favorite iPhone moment?

Author: Marne Ventura
FaceTime! For the grandchildren's first smiles, first steps, and first words.

Illustrator: Drew Feynman
I saw a story on TV news about a young boy who shot an entire film about his teddy with superpowers on his father's iPhone 5. He ended up winning prestigious international film awards and walking the red carpet (with his teddy).

Art Director: Violet Lemay
I'll never forget the first time I heard my baby's voice transmitted through any electronic device: "Hi, Mom!" through an iPhone!

Designer: Beatriz Juarez
After begging my mom to get an iPhone, she realized she could see me in real time on the other side of the screen. She thought that just happened in *Star Trek*!

Copy Chief: Michele Suchomel-Casey
When I realized that I now had a camera with me at all times, allowing me to capture spur-of-the-moment shots.

Library of Congress Cataloging-in-Publication Data
Names: Ventura, Marne, author. | Glass, Simon, illustrator.
Title: Awesome minds : the creators of the iPhone / by Marne Ventura ; art by Simon Glass (aka Drew Feynman)
Description: New York : duopress [2017] | Audience: Ages 7–10. | Audience: Grades 4 to 6.
| Description based on print version record and CIP data provided by publisher; resource not viewed.
Identifiers: LCCN 2016021426 (print) | LCCN 2016017765 (ebook) | ISBN 9781938093784 (epub) | ISBN 9781938093791 (Kindle) | ISBN 9781938093777 (paper over board : alk. paper)
Subjects: LCSH: Jobs, Steve, 1955–2011—Juvenile literature. | Wozniak, Steve, 1950—Juvenile literature. | Ive, Jonathan, 1967—Juvenile literature. | Apple Computer, Inc.—History—Juvenile literature. | iPhone (Smartphone)—History—Juvenile literature. | iPad (Computer)—History—Juvenile literature. | Computer engineers—United States—Biography—Juvenile literature. | Inventors—United States—Biography—Juvenile literature. **Classification:** LCC QA76.2.J63 (print) | LCC QA76.2.J63 V46 2017 (ebook) | DDC 621.39/0922—dc23 LC record available at https://lccn.loc.gov/2016021426

Printed in China
10 9 8 7 6 5 4 3 2 1
duopress
www.duopressbooks.com

AWESOME MINDS

The Creators
of the

iPhone®

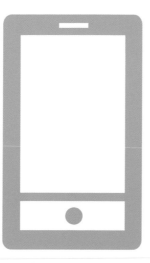

"The **best ideas** start as **conversations**."

— Jony Ive

AWESOME MINDS

The Creators
of the
iPhone®

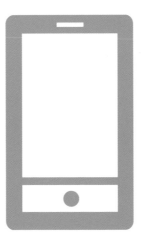

By Marne Ventura

Art by Drew Feynman

duopress

Table of Contents

A Computer
in Your Pocket

What can you do with an iPhone? Take a photo of your puppy and send it instantly to your best friend. FaceTime with your grandparents. Listen to your favorite songs. Check the weather before soccer practice. Play video games while you wait in line at the store. See what time it is all over the world. Find information for your school report. Get directions to the swim meet. Oh—and make and receive phone calls. This little electronic tool has changed the way we work, play, and live. It's a powerful and innovative computer that fits inside your pocket.

How do you know it's an iPhone? The thin rectangle with rounded corners and a glass front is sleek and simple. Touch the home button and the screen lights up. Tap or slide your fingertip across the glass to use it. You can even make it work with your voice. Flip it over and find the Apple logo.

The First Cell Phones

The first handheld portable cell phone call was made in 1973. By the time the iPhone was introduced, mobile phones had changed a lot. Here are some milestones:

- The "brick phone" (1983)—the size of a brick, it weighed two pounds.

- The flip phone (1989)— smaller than the brick, with a tiny digital display and keypad.

- The "candy bar" (1998)—named for its size and shape, with a larger digital display.

- The PalmPilot (2002)— also called a personal digital assistant (PDA), this device added email and a calendar to a phone.

- The BlackBerry (2003)—a PDA with a larger color touch screen.

In 1997, Apple chose the slogan "Think Different" for a TV ad. It was a tribute to people like Albert Einstein, Bob Dylan, and Pablo Picasso, whose science, music, and art, respectively, gave the world something new. In the same way, the iPhone gave the world a new way to communicate, find information, and have fun.

Think different.

Since the introduction of the first iPhone in 2007, more than one billion have been sold. Its creators worked hard for many years.

They collaborated. They combined ideas and inventions from people all over the world. Who were they? How did they do it?

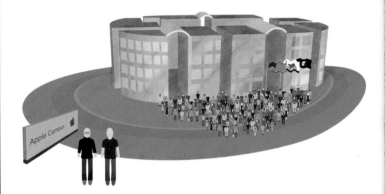

timeline

January 2007
iPhone announced; Apple drops the word "Computer" from company name

October 2001
First iPod—
"1,000 songs in your pocket"

September 2007
iPod touch—
Multi-Touch display and built-in Wi-Fi

January 2005
iPod shuffle—
the smallest iPod

July 2008
iPhone 3G—
twice as fast, half the price

Apple Campus, California.

Inventions from all over the world resulted in the creation of the iPhone.

June 2009
iPhone 3GS—
faster, longer
battery life,
better camera

June 2010
iPhone 4—
glass front and
back, stainless
steel frame,
better camera

September 2010
New iPod touch—
Retina Display,
FaceTime, HD
video recording,
and Game Center

October 2011
iPhone 4s—
better camera, Siri,
iCloud storage

September 2012
iPhone 5—faster,
aluminum, larger
Retina Display

September 2013
iPhone 5s and
iPhone 5c—faster,
Touch ID fingerprint

September 2014
iPhone 6 and iPhone
6 Plus—Retina HD
Display, Apple Pay,
Health app

September 2015
iPhone 6s and
iPhone 6s Plus—
faster, 3D Touch,
Live Photos

September 2016
iPhone 7 and iPhone
7s are released.
They come with
stereo sound and
new cameras

Insanely Great

Steve Jobs in seventh grade

Steven Paul Jobs was born on February 24, 1955, in San Francisco, California. He was a smart, curious child. He learned to read before kindergarten. Steve sometimes misbehaved at school. He had trouble making friends. He wasn't a good student until fourth grade, when his teacher got him to study by bribing him with candy bars and money. After that, his test scores were so high that he skipped fifth grade.

But when he turned 11, he no longer liked his school. Steve was already awkward socially and now he was a year younger than everyone. Instead of being put into a gifted program, he was simply thrown in

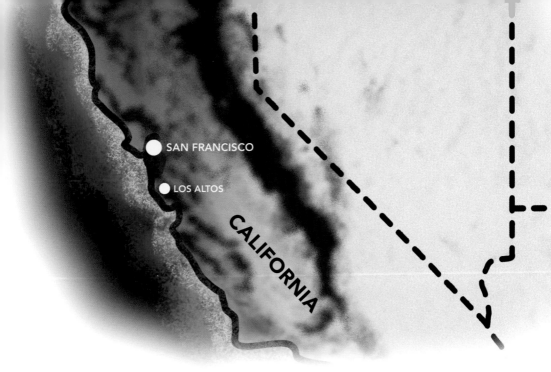

SAN FRANCISCO

LOS ALTOS

CALIFORNIA

with older kids. There were groups of rough kids who got into fights to the point that police were called in. Steve was bullied by some of these kids. Steve told his parents he wouldn't go back. They knew how strong-willed Steve could be, so they moved to Los Altos, California. Steve's new home was in an area where many technology companies started. One neighbor was an engineer. He liked to work on electronics projects in his garage. Steve loved to watch him work. He was fascinated by electronics. In high school, his favorite subjects were math and science.

Electronics

Electronics is the branch of physics that deals with electrons. Electrons are particles with a negative charge that travel around the nucleus of an atom. Devices that use electrical circuits, such as TVs and computers, are called electronics.

After high school, Steve attended Reed College in
Portland, Oregon. In less than a year he dropped out.
He didn't want to go to the classes the college required.
He wanted to do things his own way. Steve stayed at Reed,
though. The dean of students let him go to classes that
interested him. He studied calligraphy and Buddhism.
He became a vegetarian. He lived with friends at an
apple farm south of Portland.

Steve's parents did their best to help him succeed. His dad was a machinist. He liked to build things with tools and work on cars. He spent a lot of time with Steve. He taught Steve to build things well and make them beautiful—even the parts that didn't show. Like his father, Steve loved good craftsmanship. In the years to come, Steve's passion was creating electronic tools that were "insanely great, inside and out."

Calligraphy

Steve studied calligraphy, the art of making beautiful letters with pen and ink, because he found it fun and interesting. He didn't know it would be useful. Years later, he used his knowledge to create the fonts for Macintosh computers.

The Jobs Family

Steve's birth parents were students at the University of Wisconsin. Joanne Schieble was not finished with college and not married to Abdulfattah Jandali. She decided to give their baby up for adoption. Joanne moved to San Francisco to find parents for the child. She wanted her child to be raised by college graduates. One couple agreed but at the last minute decided they wanted a girl. Paul and Clara Jobs adopted Steve a few days after his birth. They were not college graduates, but they promised Joanne they would send Steve to a good college. When Steve was five years old, Paul and Clara adopted a girl they named Patty. Steve was very loyal and grateful to Paul and Clara Jobs. It bothered him when people called them his "adoptive parents." He corrected them, saying, "They're my parents."

MIDDLESEX UNIVERSITY

LONDON

HOXTON SQUARE

BUCKINGHAM PALACE

RIVER THAMES

Meanwhile, in London...

On February 27, 1967, the year that Steve entered seventh grade, Jonathan Paul Ive was born in London, England. Like Steve, "Jony" grew up around tools and workshops. His father, Michael, was a silversmith and design teacher. Jony liked to take things apart to see how they worked. He was always building things, like an obstacle course for his hamster. He was also a talented artist. Jony's father saw that his son was unusually good at designing and building. When Jony was in high school, his dad asked a design

Industrial Design

Jony's father was chosen by the British Education Ministry to oversee the teaching of woodwork, metalwork, and cooking education. Michael Ive wanted shop classes to be more than fun and easy. He wanted students to learn industrial design, the process of studying, planning, and creating a product that is beautiful, useful, and well made.

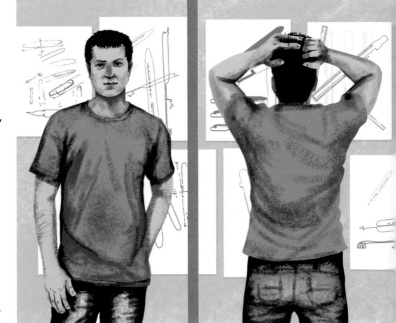

company to look at Jony's work. The company was so impressed that they agreed to pay his college fees if he would work for them afterward.

After college, Jony began work as an industrial designer. He designed pens, phones, hearing aids, and even toilets. Jony loved his work. But often, his customers asked him to change his designs. Because of the changes, the products were not as good as they could be. Jony was frustrated. Like Steve, Jony only wanted to create things that were "insanely great."

Macintosh

Before college, Jony didn't like working with computers. He worried that he wasn't good at technology. At college he used an Apple Macintosh for the first time. Jony loved it! He was impressed by the design. He felt that he and the designers were somehow connected.

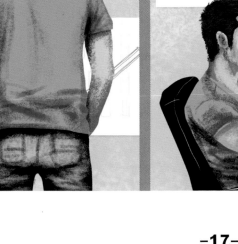

Silicon Valley

The area where the Jobs family lived is the center for technology business in the United States. It got its name from silicon, the material that is used to make computer chips. Electronic circuits are embedded into tiny wafers of silicon.

<u>Back to Silicon Valley</u>

In the spring of 1974, Steve returned home to find a job. His interest in electronics led him to Atari, a company that made a popular video game called *Pong*. At the time, it was not unusual for college students to grow their hair long and wear ripped jeans. That is how Steve looked when he went to ask for a job. He didn't even take a shower or wear shoes. He said he wouldn't leave until he was hired. The man in charge was impressed with Steve's determination and put him to work. He could see that this eccentric young man was not going to take no for an answer.

Steve spent his free time with a neighborhood friend, Steve Wozniak. They liked to play pranks, listen to the Beatles and Bob Dylan, and most of all, design and build electronic devices.

A Computer Genius

Steve Wozniak, born on August 11, 1950, was the son of an engineer. "Woz" loved electronics as a child and built his first computer when he was 13 years old. After inventing the first personal computer and starting Apple with Steve Jobs, Woz went back to college and finished his degree. Woz left Apple in 1985 and shared his passion for engineering with young learners and their teachers. He "adopted" his local school district and made sure students had new computers. He helped students learn to use them. Woz was also the founding sponsor of the Tech Museum and Children's Discovery Museum of San Jose. Steve Jobs once said of Woz, "He was the first person I met that knew more about electronics and computers than I did at the time."

The Birth of the Personal Computer

Before this time, computers were for large businesses and governments. They were huge, expensive, and complicated to use. In the 1970s, the invention of the microprocessor made it possible to create a computer that was small enough to fit on a desk.

Woz designed a computer using this new technology. He and Steve belonged to a group called the Homebrew Computer Club. Members were people who enjoyed electronics as a hobby and got together to show each other their work. Woz wanted to give the design of the new computer to the other club members. Steve knew that Woz's design was brilliant. He also knew that the members of the club would pay for it. Steve predicted that other people would pay, too. He convinced Woz to make and sell his computer instead of giving away the design.

▤ ENIAC

The first digital computer, the ENIAC (which stands for Electronic Numerical Integrator and Computer), was built during World War II to help the US Army solve math problems. It cost $450,000 to build. It used as much power in a day as most homes used in a week and filled a 30-foot by 50-foot room.

Steve and Woz were about to start what would become the most valuable company in the world. Woz was a gifted engineer. Steve was a natural leader and business manager. Soon their collaboration was going to bring the power of computers into the everyday lives of people everywhere.

⊞ Microprocessor

The microprocessor is the brain of an electronic device. The first microprocessor was about the size of a pinhead, and it contained 2,300 transistors. The microprocessor in the iPhone 6 is about the size of four postage stamps and contains two billion transistors.

Apple Computer

Why did Steve and Woz name their new company Apple? Steve had just come back from his favorite apple farm in Oregon. Also, the name "Apple" would come before their competition, Atari, in the phone book. Steve thought the name sounded fun.

Apple

Steve and Woz scraped together enough money to build their first computer. When the owner of one of the first retail computer stores saw it, he told Steve he would buy 50 of them for $500 each. Steve and Woz couldn't believe it; $25,000 was about as much as Woz made in a year, working as a full-time engineer!

Garage Start-ups

Steve and Woz are not the only ones to start a big company in a little garage. The Walt Disney Studio was started in the garage belonging to Walt's uncle Robert in North Hollywood in 1923. Jeff Bezos started Amazon in his garage in Bellevue, Washington, in 1994. And Google began in a garage near Stanford University in 1998.

The Jobs household was now home to a busy company. Steve's father moved his workshop out of the garage to make way for Steve and Woz. Steve's mother answered the phones, and Steve's sister, Patty, helped put the computer parts together. A friend of Steve's, who did the bookkeeping, slept on their living room couch.

Computer in a Book

Steve and Woz called their first computer the Apple I. Within a year, they were working on a better computer, called the Apple II. Steve introduced it at a conference in San Francisco. By this time, they had enough money to move out of Steve's garage and into an office building. Business partners began to invest in Apple. Sales were rising. Steve and Woz were now working with a team of designers.

PARC

Three of the new ideas that inspired Steve and his team to make better computers were developed at the Palo Alto Research Center (PARC). One was the graphical user interface (GUI), which used icons, or pictures on the screen, instead of text.

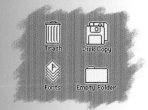

They were inspired by new inventions in technology around the world. In 1983, Steve said he would someday make a computer that would be shaped like a book that people could learn to use in 20 minutes and carry around with them. This computer would also use a "radio link" to communicate with larger databases without having to be hooked up to anything. Nobody knew it at the time, but that idea would later turn into the iPad, released 27 years later.

Second was the use of a computer mouse to control a cursor or pointer. Third was a network—the connection letting computers share information.

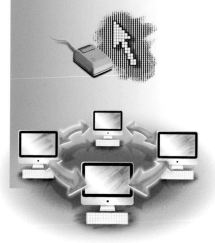

Transitions

When Steve and Woz first started Apple, Steve got to do things his own way. Now, Apple was owned by investors. A team of people ran the company. Steve wasn't always in control.

In 1985, Steve wanted to improve Apple's Macintosh computers. John Sculley, who was named the head of Apple when the company was sold to investors, wanted to keep making more Apple IIs. The people in charge sided with Sculley. They took away most of Steve's responsibilities. So Steve left Apple.

At the same time, Jony Ive was working as a designer in London. The head designer at Apple had met Jony a few years earlier. He had seen Jony's design work and offered Jony a job. But Jony had promised to work for the company that paid for his college. In 1992, the head designer at Apple went to London and asked Jony again. This time Jony said yes. He moved to San Francisco and went to work as an industrial designer for Apple Computer.

Sales were down at Apple, and the company had a new CEO, named Gil Amelio. He wanted to sell more Macintosh computers, but he needed better software. Steve Jobs now owned a company that made the kind of software that Apple needed. Steve missed working at Apple. He still wanted to make "insanely great" Macintosh computers. When Apple offered to buy Steve's software company, Steve agreed. He came back to work at Apple. Soon he was in charge again.

NEXT and Pixar

The company that Steve started after leaving Apple made computers for businesses and schools. An English engineer named Tim Berners-Lee invented the World Wide Web using one of Steve's NEXT computers. Steve also bought a computer graphics company from George Lucas, the maker of the *Star Wars* movies. He named it Pixar. In 1995, Pixar and Disney made the movie *Toy Story*.

__Kindred Spirits__

In 1997, as the new head of Apple, Steve wanted his
employees to focus on making a few awesome products.
He met with them to find out about their projects—and
he canceled a lot of projects. Steve was thinking of hiring a
new designer. He wanted the best designer he could find.

He had a few people in mind, but these designers were from outside companies.

By then, Jony Ive had been at Apple for five years. He was head of industrial design. He worried that Apple might go out of business or be bought by another company. He wasn't sure he wanted to stay. On the day that Jony and Steve met for the first time, Jony had a letter ready. The letter said he was quitting his job at Apple.

What happened at their first meeting was a big surprise to both Steve and Jony. They liked each other. Steve asked Jony about the designs in the lab. He saw that Jony shared his passion for doing things right. Jony saw that Steve would make his designs without compromises. They were both so excited that on that very same day they started working together on an idea that became the iMac. It was the beginning of a 15-year collaboration to make "insanely great" products.

A Creative Team

Jony and Steve worked together with a team of engineers and software programers to create the iMac, the MacBook, the iPod, the iPhone, and the iPad.

1980s

Record
Player

1990s

Tapes

CDs

<u>Music</u>

In 1995, scientists in Germany discovered a way to make
digital sound files, called MP3s, that could be played on
computers and shared over the Internet. Before the 1990s,
people bought vinyl records that spun on a turntable.
A needle on an arm touched the spinning disk to create
sound. Next, music was recorded on magnetic tapes.
By the 1990s, music was sold on compact discs (CDs). Most

vinyl records, tapes, or CDs had about a dozen songs, usually by the same artist, so you couldn't buy just one song. Artists got paid for their music when people bought their records, tapes, or CDs.

In 1999, an Internet program called Napster was created. The program let people transfer songs from CDs to computers and share them over the Internet. Suddenly, people got the songs they wanted for free. Musicians were angry because they weren't getting paid for their work. But many people used Napster. It was easy to get music without going to a store. People didn't have to buy twelve songs in order to get the one song they wanted.

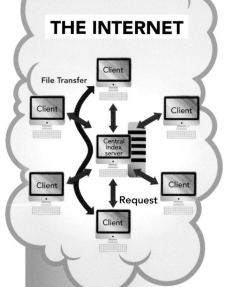

THE INTERNET

Internet and World Wide Web

In the 1960s, scientists at the Massachusetts Institute of Technology (MIT) invented the Internet when they found a way to link computers in different locations and share data. In 1989, a system of linked pages, called the World Wide Web, was created. As personal computers became popular, people used the Internet to get to the World Wide Web. The network that inspired Steve when he visited PARC in 1979 became a reality.

What's the "i" for?

The iMac was the first product released after Steve returned to Apple. The "i" stands for "Internet" and also for "individual" ("I" as in me) and "imagination." The tradition continued with iTunes, iPod, iPhone, and iPad.

Just as Steve knew that people would pay for Woz's computer, he knew there was a business opportunity with digital music. He believed customers would pay for music if they could get single songs, for a fair price, easily. And for his idea to work, musicians needed to be paid.

▣ ▥ timeline

2000
Apple buys SoundJam and creates iTunes Main feature: "1,000 songs in your pocket"

2001
iTunes introduced with first iPod

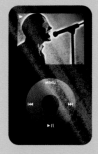

October 2005
iTunes adds music videos

September 2006
iTunes adds movies and video games

January 2010
iPad introduced

March 2011
iPad 2 announced. Main features: front and rear cameras

March 2012
New iPad 3 announced. Main feature: Hi-res Retina Display

October 2012
iPad mini and 4th generation iPad

October 2013
iPad Air. Thinner and lighter, with Retina Display

October 2014
iPad Air 2 and iPad mini 3. Main features: faster and Touch ID

2015
First Apple Watch sold

September 2015
iPad Pro

One Thousand Songs in Your Pocket

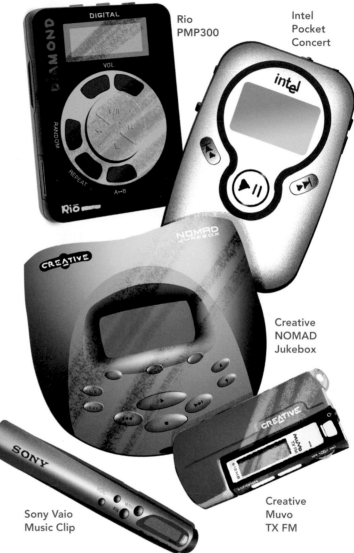

Rio PMP300

Intel Pocket Concert

Creative NOMAD Jukebox

Creative Muvo TX FM

Sony Vaio Music Clip

The first portable MP3 player came out in 1998. It was the size of a deck of cards, held 30 minutes of music, and cost $250.

In the next year, more companies made MP3 players. They were heavy, boxy, expensive, and short on memory. Steve knew he could make a better player. He asked Jony and his team to come up with something great.

The team used new technology—a 1.8-inch-diameter drive that held thousands of songs. This was smaller than the 2.5-inch drives in the existing players. Jony's design was ultra simple. He chose white for the pocket-sized rectangle and a simple wheel for making selections. It took a long time to convince Steve that white was the best color for the iPod. Jony's choice of white and his super-simple design were used in many future Apple products.

♫ **You'll See**

Not everyone foresaw the huge success of the iPod. When Jony called his dad in 2001, he said, "It'll have a thousand songs, Dad." Mike Ive answered, "Who wants a thousand songs?" Jony said, "You'll see."

Steve announced the iPod to reporters on October 23, 2001, at the Apple offices. It cost $499. Despite the iPod's many awesome features, it had some drawbacks. Users had to transfer music from a CD to a Macintosh computer, and then from the computer to the iPod. It wasn't yet possible to simply buy songs directly from the Internet, using only an iPod.

iPod Ad

Apple has a history of "insanely great" advertisements. One famous TV commercial showed a silhouette of a person against a brightly colored background. The only detail was a white iPod in one hand and white earbuds in place as the person danced to fun music.

iTunes Store

Early in 2000, Steve found a program called SoundJam. It let computer users find and play digital music. Steve bought the program from the company that made it and hired its creators to work at Apple. He changed the name to iTunes. He used it to build an online library of music.

Packaging

Steve and Jony worked to design the perfect packages for their products. They wanted customers opening their new iPods and iPhones to enjoy the experience. Cases are sleek and simple, like the products. They're made of high-quality materials. Many Apple customers keep the packaging because it's too nice to throw away.

Next, Steve met with record companies. He worked out deals with them so that artists would get paid when people downloaded songs. In 2003, the iTunes Store opened. Music lovers could use their iPods to download songs for 99 cents each. It was easy, fast, and inexpensive. People didn't need to go to music stores and buy CDs. Musicians got paid for their work. It was a smart solution to a big problem.

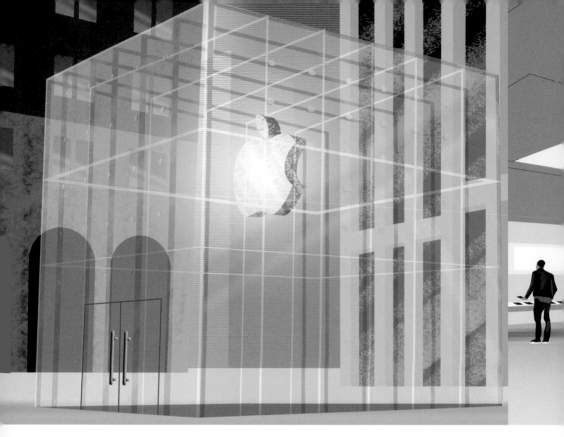

The Apple Store

Just Apple

At the beginning of 2007, Steve dropped the word "Computer" from the company name, changing it to simply Apple. He wanted the name of the company to show it was now in the business of computers and music. Soon phones and television would be added.

In 2000, Steve was unhappy with the way retail stores handled the sale of Apple products. Sometimes the displays didn't look nice. Many were in big-box stores next to televisions and kitchen appliances. Often the salespeople didn't know about the products. Steve wanted people to understand how the products could help them. He wanted people to learn how "insanely great" the products were. He decided to create his own chain of stores.

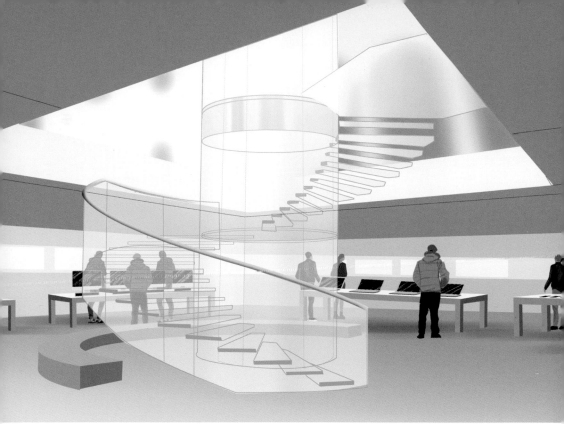

Steve's design team made stores where people learn about Apple products by touching, feeling, and using them. They created clean, beautiful spaces where customers are welcome to stay for as long as they want, check their email, surf the Web, or listen to music. Apple stores have classes for new computer users or for kids. There is a Genius Bar at the back of the store where people can ask questions.

Design Studio

Jony's design studio is like an Apple Store. Its walls are glass. There are rows of wooden tables where the team works on models of projects. There's loud music playing—Jony's favorite is techno.

GPS

The Global Positioning System is a network of satellites that send information from space to Earth. iPhones use GPS signals to give directions. GPS signals used to be scrambled so only the military could use them. President Bill Clinton allowed the signals to be unscrambled in May of 2000 so that everyone could use GPS.

Touch Sensitive

In July of 2002, Apple came out with a better iPod. It had a touch-sensitive wheel instead of a mechanical one, and it worked with Windows PC computers as well as Macs. It had a backlit screen and touch-sensitive buttons. By the end of that year, 600,000 iPods were sold. Before the iPod, most electronic

Touch-Screen Technology

A touch screen is a layer of glass coated with an electricity conductor. A human finger also conducts electricity, so when it touches the screen it changes the electric field. The computer uses this information to respond. Multi-touch technology allows a user to use more than one touch, for example, using a thumb and a finger at the same time.

technology was controlled with a key-board or stylus. The iPod changed the way people used handheld devices by introducing touch controls. Jony wanted to design and make products that "asked to be touched." Steve wanted his products to be user-friendly. Now they could make a better handheld device using touch-screen technology.

iPhone Goes on Sale

Apple announced that sales of the first iPhones would start on Friday, June 29, 2007, at 6 p.m. Eager customers lined up in front of Apple Stores as early as Tuesday. In New York, hundreds camped out in lawn chairs and sleeping bags. They brought umbrellas for the rain and the summer heat. The line wrapped around several blocks. People played Scrabble, ordered take-out food, and typed on their laptops as they waited.

Since the 1980s, handheld mobile phones had gotten smaller, lighter, and less expensive. They could be used for email and as a calendar, in addition to making phone calls.

Steve and Jony knew they could make a better phone. They wanted a design

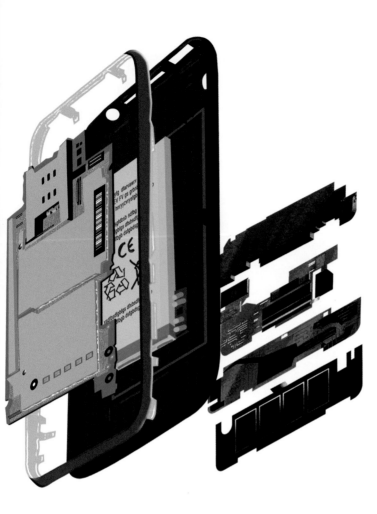

that was super simple, without a lot of buttons and keys. They thought it should be beautiful and easy to use. The new touch-screen technology was just what they needed. Jony and his team went to work on different designs. They found a strong glass, called Gorilla Glass, to use for the front of the phone. They made it black, to look like an infinity pool.

🌐 Human Rights

iPhones are made in a factory in China. The workers are not always treated fairly. The leaders at Apple often visit China to see if factory conditions are fair. They look for ways to improve life for the workers. They created a program called SEED to help educate them. Workers can take free courses to learn English, computer use, life skills, and more.

The iPhone

The product that Steve and Jony came up with combined an iPod with touch controls, a new kind of mobile phone, and an Internet device. It was different

iPod   Phone   Internet

Steve's and Jony's Styles

Steve was good at getting up in front of people and making presentations. He liked to save one important bit of information until the end. Then he would say, "And one more thing…" and surprise the crowd. Steve liked to take credit for his "insanely great" products. Jony is the opposite. He doesn't like to be the center of attention. He doesn't like to get up and talk in front of a crowd. When he does, he always shares the credit for his designs with his team.

than any other electronic device at the time. Apple sold four million iPhones (priced at $499 or $599) during the first year.

MATRIX
MASTER **PRO**

0.2

VIRTUAL SPREADSHEET

<u>There's an App for That</u>

After the first personal computers came out, developers began to create software for them. They made word processors for writing documents, spreadsheets for keeping track of numbers, and games to play. These programs, also called applications, let people use their com-

MATRIX MASTER PRO 0.2
DISC 1

MATRIX MASTER PRO 0.2 SHEET
DISC 2
VIRTUAL SPREADSHEET

puters in many ways. The software was on a CD. It came in a box with an instruction book. Software was often expensive.

The Internet and the World Wide Web made it easier and less expensive for computer users to get applications. Instead of putting software on a physical disc that had to be bought at a store or sent through the mail, people could buy and download applications online.

☺ Becoming Part of the Culture

The phrase "There's an app for that" became popular in 2009, after Apple ran a TV commercial showing some of the many things you can do with iPhone apps. Today, there are apps for practicing mathematics, writing stories, seeing how you'd look with different hair, or taking awesome pictures and videos.

The design team at Apple went a step further with the iPhone. Since this new device was actually a tiny computer, it could run applications, nicknamed "apps," to do all kinds of things. The team created iOS, an operating system that developers use to make apps for playing games, keeping

calendars, tracking health, finding directions, and thousands of other things.

Then they created the App Store. People can use their iPhones to buy apps using an Internet connection. Like songs in the iTunes Store, apps often cost 99 cents. Apps can be downloaded immediately, so there's no waiting for a package to be shipped.

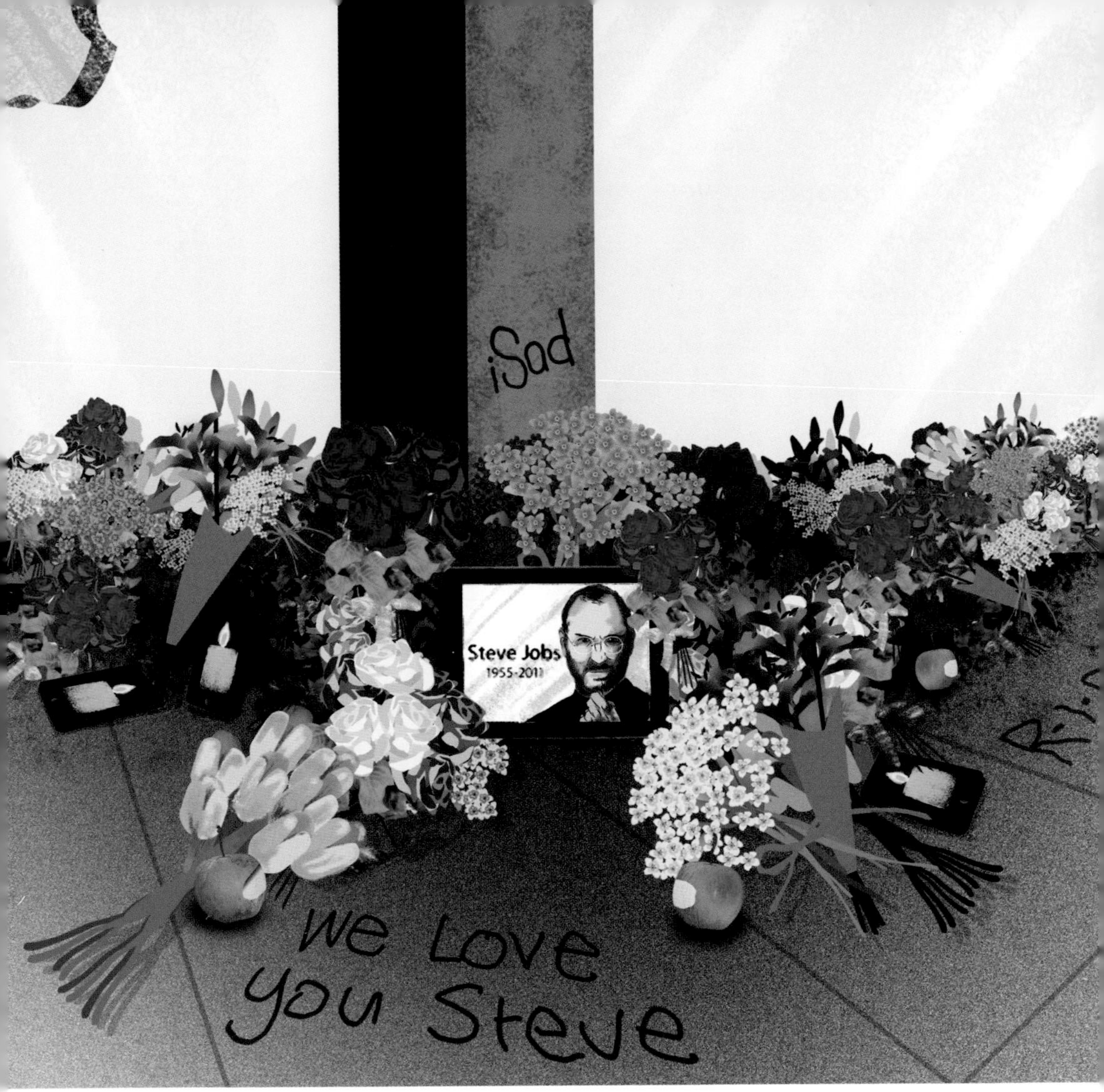
iSad
Steve Jobs
1955-2011
We Love you Steve

The iPhone Today

Sadly, Steve Jobs passed away on October 5, 2011, after an eight-year battle with cancer. Around the world, people put flowers in Apple Store doorways to show their appreciation for the man who changed their lives by working so hard to make "insanely great" electronic tools.

Jony Ive spoke at Steve's memorial service. He said Steve "constantly questioned, 'Is this good enough? Is this right?'

And despite all his successes, all his achievements, he never presumed, he never assumed, that he would get there in the end. And when the ideas didn't come, and when the prototypes failed, it was with great intent, with faith, he decided to believe he would eventually make something great."

Jony lost a good friend when Steve died. But he and his team are still designing new electronic tools. In 2015, they came out with the Apple Watch, an electronic wristwatch that has many of the features of an iPhone. Jony became head of software, working to make iOS the best it can be. He's also in charge of designing Apple Stores around the world. In Cupertino, California, Jony's design ideas are being used for new Apple office buildings.

Can you imagine life today without the iPhone? Because of Steve Jobs's and Jony Ive's ability to "think different" and their many years of collaboration, our everyday lives are vastly better in many ways. Because of their passion for "insanely great" tools, we can play, work, communicate, and learn, using a computer-phone that fits in our pockets.

Are iPhones and iPods always awesome? Some parents wonder if spending too much time using an iPhone can be harmful to their children. Education and child-development experts say that moderation is very important. Spending most of the day playing games on an iPhone is not healthy. But, for school-age children who get plenty of exercise, spend time playing with friends, and do hands-on activities and hobbies, iPhones and iPods could be great tools for communicating and learning.

Teamwork

This book focuses on how Steve Jobs and Jonathan Ive worked to create the iPod and the iPhone. But both devices were built by the hard work and ingenuity of many people. Some of the other talented people who helped design and develop the iPod are:

•Tony Fadell. Senior vice president of the iPod Division at Apple. He created the concept and initial design of the iPod in 2001.

•Jon Rubinstein. On a trip to Japan in 2001, he found the tiny 1.8-inch hard disk drive that made the iPod possible.

•Michael Dhuey. The engineer who worked with Tony Fadell to develop the hardware and battery for the original iPod in 2001.

•Tim Wasko. An interface designer.

•Vinnie Chieco. A freelance copywriter who had the idea for the name "iPod". He got the idea from a line in the movie *2001*: "Open the pod bay door, HAL."

•Kane Kramer. An English inventor who patented the idea for a plastic portable digital music player in 1979. His patent expired when MP3 players hit the market.

•Bart Andre. Joined Apple in 1992. In 2013, he had more patents to his name than any other Apple designer.

The US government awarded Apple a patent for the iPhone in 2012. To receive a patent, inventors need to prove they have made something that didn't exist until they thought it up. Others cannot make the same invention without the inventor's permission, once it is patented. This is the team of awesome minds that are listed on the patent as inventors of the iPhone:

- Barley K. Andre
- Daniel J. Coster
- Daniele De Iuliis
- Richard P. Howard
- Jonathan P. Ive
- Steve Jobs
- Duncan Robert Kerr
- Shin Nishibori
- Matthew Dean Rohrback
- Douglas B. Satzger
- Calvin Q. Seid
- Christopher J. Stringer
- Eugene Antony Whang
- Rico Zorkendorfer

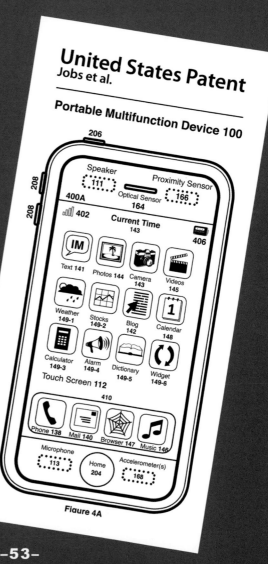

📰 GLOSSARY

big-box store Retail store that occupies a big amount of physical space and offers many different products to its customers.

Buddhism The religion and spiritual philosophy founded by Gautama Buddha between the sixth and fourth centuries BCE that teaches the detachment from desires and one's self.

circuit The system of conductors through which electric current moves.

collaboration The act of working with other people to achieve a goal.

hydroelectric Related to the creation of electricity by water in motion.

investor A person or company that puts money into something to turn a profit.

microprocessor The unit that contains and controls all the functions of a computer.

software All the programs, information, and instructions used by a computer.

techno music A style of electronic music born in Detroit that has a fast beat and lack of melody.

BOOKS

Hagar, Erin, and Paige Garrison. *Awesome Minds: The Inventors of LEGO® Toys*. Baltimore, MD: duopress, 2016.

MacLeod, Elizabeth, Frieda Wishinsky, and Qin Leng. *A History of Just About Everything: 180 Events People and Inventions That Changed the World*. Toronto, ON: Kids Can Press, 2013.

100 Inventions That Made History. New York, NY: DK Publishing, 2014.

Powell, Jillian. *Greatest Inventions of All Time*. London, UK: Wayland, 2016.

Robinson, Sir Tony. *Tony Robinson's Weird World of Wonders: Funny Inventions*. New York, NY: Macmillan Children's Books, 2013.

Ventura, Marne. *The 12 Biggest Breakthroughs in Computer Technology*. North Mankato, MN: Peterson Publishing, 2015.

WEBSITES

http://inventivekids.com
http://scienceofeverydaylife.com
https://kids.usa.gov/teens/science/scientists/index.shtml
http://www.factmonster.com/ipka/A0004637.html
http://www.enchantedlearning.com/inventors/

◻ INDEX